Diana Button

Wakes of Joy

Poems

Bibliographic information of the German National Library: The Deutsche Nationalbibliothek catalogs this publication in the Deutsche Nationalbibliographie. More bibliographic information can be found on the internet: http//dnb.ddb.de

Published by BoD · Books on Demand GmbH, Überseering 33, 22297 Hamburg, bod@bod.de

Printed by Druck: Libri Plureos GmbH, Friedensallee 273, 22763 Hamburg

ISBN: 978-3-7693-8975-3

For Gangaji, the lineage of Ramana Maharshi, and the ever-present silence that calls us home.

Preface

A single moment—
a breath, a pause, a stillness—
and something within us stirs.

Perhaps it is recognition. Perhaps remembering.

There is a joy not bound by circumstance, a stillness that does not waver, a presence that has never left. It moves like ripples across water, like the wake of a boat long gone, yet still shaping the surface.

This collection is an invitation—an unfolding into that wake of joy, into the waves of awakening. It does not ask you to search, but rather to rest, to listen, to remember.

As you read these poems, may you find moments of stillness in their movement, and glimpses of the boundless in their brevity. May they be a mirror, reflecting something that was never lost.

Welcome to *Wakes of Joy*.

The First Ripples

Gangaji, Your Existence

Gangaji, your existence

is a compass in my palm—

always at hand, pointing true north.

I listen, and the way ahead

lights up, right here,

where I stand.

You take my hand,

I feel your pulse. Our hearts join.

In that moment, I know:

I've always known.

Welcome home—

to the holy company of Self.

Who Am I Really?

I lie down on the lawn,
allow this body to rest,
allow this mind to just be.

Thoughts continue, but nothing is new—
just the same old not-so-golden oldies,
stories and rote:
The Mistaken Zygote
The Ugly Duckling
The Lost Child
She Who Will Never Belong
The Shameful One.

Verbs, nouns, and pronouns swirl,
twisting, unwinding, tumbling down—
back to where they began,
back into the dance with grass shoots and roots,
with worm and soil—

feeding billions of micro-beings

who, all the while, have been keeping

Everything alive.

Where do I begin? Where do I end?

What in me is not also in you,

in the earth, in the universe?

What in the universe, in the earth, in you,

is not also in me?

Air streams into lungs,

blood fills the bellies of thirty-seven trillion cells.

Mind is lost for words at last—

There is just this tremendous

R E V E R E N C E

Revelation No-Thing

No-thing stands apart

from this vastness,

from the boundless One

we have never left.

Confusion rises.

Fear stirs—

yet nothing is lost.

Even the idea of no-thing

fades,

dissolving

back into the eternal

wholeness

we are.

Noise and Other Sound

Sacredness is always here, but I look away,

distracted by the mind's endless chatter—

preoccupations, worry, fretting,

concerned with comfort, image, need,

the rituals of falling short

in a well-rehearsed, endless dance.

I can stop. Will I?

What will it take? Willingness? Devotion?

Blind faith? The force of God?

Rumi would have Love

pull me by the ears,

sprinkle holy water on my face,

wash away the impulses

that mislead this soul—

perhaps gently, perhaps with force,

but always with tenderness.

Yes. I say "Yes."

Each day, I repeat, "Yes,"

and still forget—

like lines for a play.

Now I vow:

"I will stay true to the word."

How could I not?

Three little letters,

but powerful enough to shape my days.

(In German, "Ja." In Italian, "Sì" Just two!)

Or perhaps it could be just one sound—

a simple /ah/

that echoes through every breath.

The Longing Within

Give your whole life to it,

give your whole self to it.

No more resisting—let it grow,

expand,

until it knocks at your heart:

Let me in, let me in!

I belong to you.

You belong to me.

We are longing itself—

returned,

rightly requited.

Heart within Heart,

within Heart,

within—

the Heart of all Hearts.

The Names We Call Ourselves

I am Fearful,

I am Vulnerable,

I am Worthless,

I am Unhappy,

I am Doubtful,

I am Fearless,

I am Invincible,

I am Worthy,

I am Confident...

First name: FVWUDFIWC

Surname: CWIFDUWVF

Names with no meaning,

Names that lead to nothing,

And so I shed them, one by one,

like old skin falling away,

leaving only light.

Candle On a Drafty Sill

I am trembling like a candle

on a drafty sill; shivering

in "too-thin" skin

on "too frail" legs.

Yet within, cells spin wild with glee.

Mind may blow and blow

at the fearful one, trying to snuff her out;

lights may dim and darkness enter in.

But here I stay, trembling

just as I am—

keeping

vigil

on this drafty sill.

Note to Self

As traffic slows

in the fast lane of thought,

a bump, a jolt—

mind's sure road falters.

I see a figure on the curb,

beckoning me over,

telling me to stop.

'I am Truth,' it says,

opens the door,

slides onto my lap,

grabs the wheel,

climbs up my arms,

and settles in my heart.

You may wonder who or what Truth is—

to be honest, I can't say.

But next time you're driving

in the fast lane of thought,

slow down, look out—

Truth will be standing there,

waiting,

inviting you to stop,

and let it take you home.

The Presence of Who

What is it that enables these hands to throw back

the sheets, and set these feet, one after the other,

into the cool embrace of day?

How do I leave this cosy nest,

wrapped in warmth,

cloaked in another's soft, sleepy body,

and face this indifferent weather?

Perhaps there is no answer to the *What* or the

How,

but the *Who*…

Who?

I have no name for you,

and yet, here you are—

moving me,

calling me,

drawing me to answer,

to bow before your quiet majesty:

The light of the sun.

The breath of dawn.

The wren's first song.

And the hot lemon drink slipping down

this dry, thirsty throat,

like the gift of life itself.

All That Matters

My brain has grown plump and ripe with matter
– somewhat grey and dull –
a matter that cannot be seen.

My head has not changed shape,
my face is the same,
though age is inked around jaw, lips, and eyes.

I care not for material things, or even immaterial
ones;

I care for what truly matters,
the kind of matter that cannot be thought or
known
by a brain alone.

Refresh

We are hardwired and also soft-wired,

We can reboot the "softwire."

Unplug everything,

Slip out of hardwiring

And into the soft, open heart.

Trans Scribe

I transcribe, write down the words

spoken in Satsang.

I am not a scribe from ancient times,

but a trans-scriber,

a trans-former of spoken word into text.

This is not *creative*, you might say,

not like poetry —

but in its own way,

it trans-ports,

from trance to source,

from here to Here.

Just Suppose

Just suppose I could zoom out from this place
called 'me' and see myself—infinitesimal.

Just suppose you could zoom out from this place
called 'you' and see yourself—astronomical.

Just suppose we could zoom out from this place
called 'man' and see ourselves—equal to none

(and ninety-seven percent stardust).

The Name of the Ache

Let the ache in—

Let it ache, and ache, and ache.

And be amazed how the ache is like a tune

you once heard, now stuck in your mind,

an earworm that tortures you,

words you've never known,

sounds that meet you

in the most intimate places,

places you cannot name—

places that cannot be described.

They sing and hum and thrum,

aching, aching, aching,

with this thing you cannot name,

until it spills over, euphoric—

moaning its true name:

S w e e t   A c h e.

Remedy Within

Plasma flows like sap through trees,

sealing wounds, knitting brokenness.

Pancreas and spleen hum beneath our skin,

steadying us through sorrow, fear, and

restlessness,

tuning our bodies

to the ancient song of survival.

Trillions of cells spin,

bearing the cries, prayers, struggles,

and triumphs of those before us—

and those yet to come.

Passed down, threading us forward,

ushering us into the unknown.

Aloe soothes, cool balm upon the skin,

its green leaves steady, soft,

comforting through dark nights, cold winters.

Each leaf a quiet miracle,

a touch deep as bone.

Sea cucumbers regenerate limb by limb,

teaching us repair is slow, deliberate—

a quiet unfolding back into life.

The willow bends,

its bark holding the secret to pain's release,

its branches whispering:

"Endure. Yield. Bow, but do not break."

Blood courses like rivers in the earth,

carrying the power to restore.

It rises to seal the wound,

a tide of warmth and renewal,

every drop a story written in red,

linking us to all who came before,

to all who will follow.

We carry the remedy within us,

passed down from root and stone,

from the breath of sky, the dust of stars.

It flows through us—

a living legacy,

a current of healing, unbroken,

an undying thread that binds us

to the past,

to the future,

to all beings

who breathe with us.

This Melancholy…

…It's here.

What else is here?

A buzzing in the body—

especially in my thighs.

Spaciousness is here,

and in it,

the melancholy,

the uncertainty,

the concerns about the future,

the tension around my role, my path, my

inertia—

frozen.

Complacency.

Shame.

Inadequacy.

Laziness.

Disgrace.

I am here.

I can't be not here,

no matter what happens or how I feel,

or where I go.

I am here.

I can feel:

the chair beneath me,

my buttocks pressing,

my feet, my fingers,

the pen in my grip,

the lemon tang on my tongue.

What a gift!

Shall I return it?

Or let it radiate out?

A Seasoned Addict

A seasoned addict

knows how to scratch an itch,

knows what a human will do

for a drink,

to escape pain, discomfort,

dis-ease.

And a seasoned addict

knows how to knock

on my door.

I could open it, yet I don't.

The keys are hidden—

tucked behind the ribs in my "treasure chest."

Instead, I host a new guest:

an awakened one

who does not budge when the addict calls,

who keeps the windows latched,

the hearth untouched by this tricky one.

The seasoned addict knows how to beg,

how to argue and persuade,

how to convince me that only wine will do—

a single glass, nothing more.

Like a stray cat curling by the fire,

pleading for cream, then staying for more.

The awakened one watches, waits,

falls into a sound and sober sleep

that drives the addict insane.

I creep into the bedroom,

take the keys,

let the addict in.

The awakened one stirs,

sees the intruder and roars:

"This is not your home!"

chasing her back into the night.

Then she sits by the fire with me,

breaks bread, offers butter,

enough cream to quench

the thirst of a lioness.

The awakened one asks only this:

"Follow me."

"Even into the dark wild unknown."

I sleep by the fire,

my body stroked hot by the flames.

I hear the purr of the stray cat,

and within me,

a lioness begins to rise.

By morning, I am resolved.

By evening, the addict knocks.

I stand before the door,

the whisper of the awakened one

guiding me away from its threshold,

toward the fire inside.

The hearth glows steady, waiting.

A shift—

not resistance, but balance.

A knowing:

I need never

answer the door.

It's Friday, and all is functioning:

- Gas heating
- Solar lighting
- Water running
- Cooker cooking

Body is warm and clean,

Belly is fed,

Bills are too.

Even if the mind is blind,

Here, beauty persists, regardless.

How, then, can I serve this?

Open these eyes of mine, look, and see—

It's Friday, and all is functioning.

Call and Response

Are these cells echoes, calls of our ancestors?

Cries, prayers—struggles and triumphs—

passed down,

so I may stand here, thriving.

The cells in my hands,

cells from millennia of life,

flowing now in me, my fingers…

allowing words to metabolize with grace,

and tell of sorrows, joys, and who we truly are—

Where do my loyalties lie?

And my longings?

Am I called to pass on

all I hear and feel?

My cells speak,

and listen too.

They whisper:

be brave, kind, wise, and true.

Haven't we always been

calling and responding,

deep inside?

I Want You to Want Me

What I truly want is for longing to meet me

at the crossing of flame and forest,

where the smoke rises to meet the sky.

For Life to drum on the ribs of my chest,

a rhythm like waves breaking on rocks,

deep and steady, crashing into bone.

A heartbeat that flickers like fire against wood,

crackling through my skin,

waking every cell.

To bow down before Grace

and say: I want You to want me, too.

To hear Grace say,

I do.

By Water's Edge

It is silence,

silence I yearn—

and I wonder,

how is death?

Is it peaceful,

peaceful and light?

It is ease,

ease I yearn—

and I sink

to the depths.

Yes!

It is peaceful here.

It is lightness,

lightness I yearn—

and I bubble

up from the bottom,

back up to the light.

It is air,

air I yearn—

and I breathe:

in and out,

in and out.

It is joy,

joy I yearn—

and I smile.

I smile,

I smile.

Silence.

Hope for Our Home

I invite you to walk

barefoot on grass

when you can,

and at every crossroads

choose to follow

this less-trodden path.

Close your eyes

and feel

the softness,

the wet, wet dew,

and perceive

the many seeds

you know are there,

with slugs and worms,

a finger-poke deep

in the dirt.

Be still, and choose

this way of humility,

of respect—

for the land,

for the good,

green world,

where each step

holds hope

for our home.

The River Gives Way

This One Prayer

O blessed light,

this divine night,

take me, use me,

in whatever way you like.

This is all I seek,

for this one life.

Amen.

House of Forbidden Joy

How long will I hold on,
keep myself from being taken
by this wild, unbidden joy?

There are no keys, no locks,
no doors or walls—
yet something stands guard.

Then, a kiss on each palm,
and my arms unfold.

Knees buckle, and
I am outside, where the guard stands.

And together, we dance.

Craving the Infinite

Thirst and hunger arrive—

like homeless cats,

seeking warmth,

a hearth to curl up to,

a bowl of cream.

Thirst and hunger arrive—

like drummers without sticks,

aching for sound,

for rhythm strong enough

to make stone weep.

I arrive—

mouth wide,

ready to be consumed,

swallowed whole

into the infinite belly of being.

You May Kiss Me Now

It must be now.

I cannot wait another moment,

I am yours,

I am yours.

I have never belonged to another

(except in drunken thought)

But I am sober now –

You must claim me!

Ah, just one kiss –

All I have ever wanted.

How it burns through every desire,

into the centre of longing.

Let me melt,

Let me melt,

Let me melt,

into this one kiss,

into this One,

into This.

The Cloak and the Wind

Let me lay it down right here

on this moss-covered stone,

my cloak of countless pockets—

pockets stuffed for generations

with insecurities,

tales of human woe.

Just for an instant,

I lay it down,

drape it limp and idle

over this sacred ground.

Let longing lead me—

show me what remains

when my cloak of burdens

slips from my skin,

no longer holding the reins.

And I step forward,

cloak-less, unbound,

my body still heavy,

cold upon this earth.

Yet my spirit rises—

billows wide and seamless,

rides the wind, untethered,

blown across the endless sky.

Bashing Against the Pane

A pair of blue bottles hum around the kitchen,

unbothered as I watch,

their bodies thumping against the glass,

again and again.

I walk to the window,

open it wide, and watch

as they fly back into the room.

Perhaps some flies prefer captivity,

trapped by their hunger,

by their very name: "Housefly."

And what of me?

Am I bashing against my own glass,

my own name: "Housewife"?

Maybe it is so.

Maybe it is not so.

Or maybe—
will I simply fly?"

Knot Inside the Knot

A knot has got inside the knot

and is beginning to unwind.

The knotted-ness of generations –

the rat king of mind –

I am returned to

This:

One

single

thread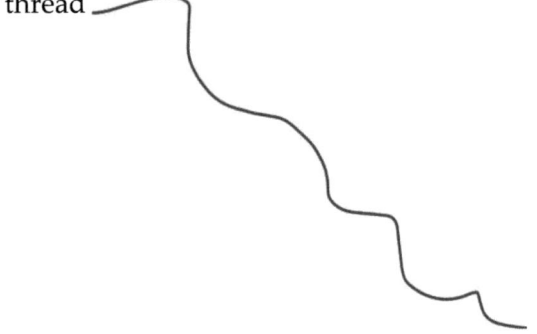

By the River of Thought

I am like a fish lured to bait,

unable to resist that glint, that pull.

One bite—and I am caught,

reeled into some juicy thought.

I know thoughts are not real—

that I cannot be hooked, caught, or devoured.

Until the thought bites.

Until it swallows me whole.

Ah, but remember this:

A thought will also let you go

when you stop luring it in,

when you stop biting back,

when you simply stop fishing.

Deeper into Yourself

If you are willing to fall

off the edge of the earth, off the brim of the sea,

off the verge of your ordered world…

You may discover

you've been holding on to nothing.

And you cannot fall off—

you can only fall deeper into yourself.

This Wild Ride That is Life

We might think we're the controller,

knowing when and how

to slow life down,

when and how

to speed life up.

But this ride that is life,

is WILD:

a spring torrent gushing

down the mountain,

ever faster, rapids and falls,

overflowing into creeks, rivers,

lakes as it rushes on to the sea.

At an eddy we might gather,

rest a while, mellow.

Then it's off again,

to where life wishes to go.

Whether we wish for this, or that, or not,

plays no role.

We are on this wild ride

called Life, and we can but flow.

Flow just wants to flow,

Life just wants to live.

All things wild and free

Just want to be

Wild and Free.

Simply going exactly where we are going,

To nowhere in particular—

endless beginnings, beginning-less ends.

Courage Is…

… to break and enter

the tiny box I am,

find that stick

of flaming potential,

and dare (even if only once)

to strike it

along the rough wall of shame…

… to let myself

burst into flame

before the entrance

of my secret hiding place…

… to radiate and reverberate,

to where it all begins—

alight in sudden knowing:

courage has no end.

Ode to Rumi

Oh, how your words roll off the page

into my ears, into my gut, down to my feet—

and gush into my heart.

Wave after wave rolls in,

blood cells swelling and spinning,

growing large and plump as eggs.

The heart becomes a greedy nest,

opening its beak wide,

letting them all in,

into its fiery depths.

How I might explode!

Then, a moment comes—

like a mass hatching,

fledglings' wings opening:

everything spilling out—

and Joy surging in!

"Let me drown" I exclaim with delight.

"Let me die in the arms of my truest Friend."

It will be my ode to Rumi.

In a Word, Yes

Yes, is saying Y e s
to willingness, to feeling
exactly what you are feeling,
not needing anything else.

Yes, is living Y e s
truly, intuitively – a promise
to be who you are
without knowing how.

Yes, is meeting Y e s,
agreeing to dare greatly
and to leap courageously
into the unknown.

Yes, is realizing Y e s
is the way through fear –
to the answer that is here,

in your heart.

Yes, is allowing Y e s,
standing firm in This,
setting yourself free
with each resounding
Y e s.

Today's Sunrise

A new book, a fresh start,

I am paying attention

to words,

to sounds,

to shapes,

and the wake the pen makes

as it sails across this page.

I look back and see

the urgency

in today's sunrise:

"You must be here for me, just for me!" it bursts.

"You must! You must! You must!"

Inspiration is endless

and won't turn off its source for anyone—

even those already out of their depth.

I surrender all hope

that salvation is anywhere

to be found.

"Sunrise beauty, precious ruby!"

And I am poured into the blazing sea.

"Oh, magnificent drowning!"

The Promise of Poetry

Let me bend your ears

like wind bending a blade of grass.

Let me fall into your eyes

like lightning from a cloud.

Let me cluster in your heart

like aphids around a bud.

Let me seep into your skin

like sap from healing trees.

Let me swell inside your mouth

like the sound of

the word

allow.

allOW

all OW

a l l O W

Don't Go Worshipping Rainbows

Don't go worshipping rainbows—

though their beauty and form are pure,

their arcs point to

the Secret of Everything,

the way

right back

to the source.

But…

Don't go worshipping rainbows

or live in awe and wonder

of their light.

Let all the worshipping free,

live and let be,

and see how the gold

you seek

Is You.

It's All a Love Affair

It's all a love affair, you know,
all a love affair.

Self in love with itself,
Self angry with itself,
Self defending itself,
Self hating itself.

And with such passion!
It has to be a love affair:
Shiva's Dance,
Christ's Heart,
Goddess in your dreams.

All a love affair!
Your worst enemies?
Your pain, anger, rage?
Other's pain, anger, rage?

Still the Beloved!

Finally, it's all the same:

Just One

True

Love

Affair.

Grand Oak

May I return here,

to you, Grand Oak, and this place by the pond,

where herons may stand, boatmen may skate,

mallards may fight, may mate.

May I return to this place,

where mosquitos bite and children shriek,

their nets coming alive with stickleback.

And again, may I return here,

to sit by the pond where lilies bloom,

breezes blow, and pollen, petals, acorns fall,

where water, pads, mud, grass,

and my hands receive all they are given.

May I, may you, may we,

simply return here again and again,

and know without knowing

how we dwell deep inside your heartwood,

and you dwell deep inside ours.

Grateful Is Too Skinny a Word

Grateful is too skinny a word

to hold the joy that grows and grows—

seedcoats inside a pomegranate,

ripe to overflowing,

tended, watered

by You.

A New To-do List

Snowflakes fall and gift me

a new to-do list – one that reads like this:

- stand still
- listen to breath breathing you
- see the fresh snow beneath you
- sense each unique flake,

   alive and fleeting, within you
- simply be

Will you accept and rest

in That?

What Remains

I lose the weight of my coat,

its seams stretched thin with history,

the echoes of old voices, the ones that told me

who I should be.

I lose the roles I played — mother, daughter,

worker, friend — and set them aside

like clothes too tight to wear.

I lose the slow creak of my bones, the stiff joints

that told me I had been here too long,

the flicker of certainty, the candle that burned

bright in my chest,

the whispers of the past,

the quiet tug of what I thought

I should be.

I lose...

and see what remains, what is still here—

what a glorious losing of all I was controlling,

and what a glorious recognition of the substance

that remains fresh and alive,

pulsating and breathing—

P　　　E　　　A　　　C　　　E

Wakes of Light

How Could I Have Guessed?

How could I have guessed

as I spun inside those clouds

that turned from grey to blacker than black,

spitting hailstones large as frogs—

that this was the way

not to death, but to life,

that those ammunition balls

were not hurled to hurt, but

to burn the rigidness

into fine and fertile ash.

How could I have guessed

that I would then be lifted up

into the same fierce storm,

to be floated back down

fresh and light as snow.

Wakes of Joy

I am keeping vigil

with a touch as watchful as a bee.

I am playing

with a heart as open as laughter.

I am growing mindful

with a mind as full as an embrace.

I am…

waking up

with poems as joyful as can be.

The Sound of Nothing

Cars passing, people talking, birds chirping,
kettle boiling, music playing, ears buzzing,
stomach rumbling, heart pumping, muscles
throbbing…

What is this?

Answer: nothing.

Nothing?

Yes, don't you hear it?

The silence beneath the noise,
the space that holds it all,
the stillness that lets the world unfold.

This Moment After the Mind Storm

I am whispering now,

no longer shouting.

Not a word, not a sound

claims this moment after the storm.

Vigilance, I thank you—

for tethering my thoughts,

for keeping past and future

in their rightful place.

Right here.

Where peace neither comes nor goes.

Where peace simply *is*.

The Light That Sees

You are the Light that sees

lightness and darkness,

like a dawn breaking the grip of night,

colour spilling into the world's quiet canvas.

You are the Light that sees

the shadows dance with the sun,

the way the earth breathes beneath your feet,

the pulse of life in every step.

You are the Light that sees

individual and cosmic consciousness,

intertwined like roots beneath the soil,

a tree stretching through time and space.

You are the Light that sees

the stars and the rivers,

the pulse of the wind and the silent sky,

and the heartbeat within.

You are the Light that sees

Itself in No-thing-ness,

where the empty space hums with potential,

where the void is full with all that is,

and all that isn't yet.

You are the Light that sees—

You are the Love,

and the Love is You,

a river of warmth flowing between us,

a current that carries us beyond all borders,

no beginning, no end.

How do I know?

Because we are not two.

You are my own Self,

I am your own Self.

We are both,

the ocean in a drop,

the drop in the ocean.

Aloneness, Not Loneliness

Here I am—alone—

Aloneness and I

get along,

never quite lonely,

though it's hard to explain.

We know how we need each other

to survive—togetherness,

a human necessity

for longevity.

But what of aloneness?

Is it also a necessity?

When another keeps us company—

a dog, a friend, the tv, the noise—

are we still alone?

In aloneness,

I find myself bursting

with life,

with a quiet, expansive aliveness

that doesn't need company

to breathe.

Humus Humblis

Humus,

ha...

ha...

ha...

Humour,

ha...

ha...

ha...

Humus,

ha...

ha...

ha...

Hum... Bliss...

a breath,

a pause—

earth laughs,

heart opens,

soul sighs.

Humus...

sings,

fertile with laughter.

Humour...

twinkles in the dirt,

spreading joy through roots and leaves.

Bliss...

not a thing,

but a moment,

a hum...

a *humus humblis*

rippling through the soil,

through the sky,

through the ocean,

through me,

through you.

In Deep

I know I am in deep

when heart sighs

and something gives inside.

When the skin

ripples over itself like the sea,

and the tiny hairs

wave bold and free,

when this head

of mine freefalls

into Life

and bobs in the ocean,

nodding:

Yes, Yes, Yes.

Poem Song

I sing to each and every one,

to those who resist, to those who blame me—

for waking them from their blissful sleep.

You call me too sweet, too small—

toss me aside or fling me in the bin.

But I will not be gone—on a whim.

Inside, you may tremble,

organs and senses quiver,

but I am not here as life support

to body, flesh, or bone.

I am the pulse of your soul, the bright dawn,

the chorus of beauty in your being.

Saying the Sayable

I can only say
that which I can say
in the way I am able
to say it.

I can only say
the sayable,
I cannot say
the unsayable.

Yet I trust
the unsayable
can and may
come through
in ways unknown
if and when
I say the sayable.

I Am Sky

I am Sky, but not the sky you may think I am.

I am a small, blue-coloured dog, a cuddly toy

who loves to be loved

and belong to this little girl.

I love her even when she pulls my tail,

wipes her snotty nose on my ears

or uses my belly to soak up tears,

whilst squeezing me much too hard.

I wonder whether I am getting loved to bits.

Perhaps I am…

coming undone—

thread by thread,

but I wouldn't want it any other way.

Retreat Is…

…deep rest, a place of nourishment,
support, guidance, encouragement—
a sanctuary where you can give up the fight,
be truly seen, exposed.

The mind's habits spill out,
running wild in the open field of light.

…setting aside phones and tablets,
teachings, practices,
letting go of strategies, methods,
and all understanding.

Thoughts of success, failure, best self, worst self,
and all other selves
gather at every edge of "you,"
and freefall into the great good luck

of simply being here—

right side up.

Echoes of the Earth

How I regret, how I regret, how I regret,

that I have not spent my life

in communion

with the sacredness of the land

I've had the privilege

to stand on.

I grieve and sob, grieve and sob, grieve and sob,

for all that is lost,

for all that has passed,

for forgotten reverence, dismissed meaning,

for all the turning away

from the offspring of creation.

And I nestle into this grief,

as I nestle down

by the roots of this oak,

where last autumn's leaves and this spring's

grass

make a fine cushion for this sore, sorry soul.

I become quiet, feel a swelling around me,

a welling below me,

and unseen words enter me

from this wondrous, wordless being:

Who says you have not lived in communion with the

sacredness of the land?

Who says it is so?

Is it your mind?

Does this mind say you have been blown

far from my roots,

far from yourself,

far from the truth of who you are?

What if I were to tell you what is truly true –

that you are the mist that caresses my feet,

the mist that gathers above the lake,

turns and swirls across the fields,

streams gleefully into the woods,

simply because it is the nature of mist

to do just that?

What if I were to tell you

that you make this land lush

along with the sun –

that your tears, your sobs,

disperse droplets

like seeds, wide and far

when you are true to yourself,

to your knowing that you

have never been separate

from the sacred land

on which you have always

been standing.

Would you believe me, or your mind?

Memo

I grew up talking to daisies on the lawn,
making countless chains and then letting
myself be tamed into many neat rows,
like the tulips in the bed out front.

I grew far from Wild Willow
and my fluffy catkin friends
who tickled my skin and made me giggle.

And I grew arrows inside this heart
once piercing in hard—
but now, with my adult bow,
I know how to aim and shoot
into every blooming thing
(hypothetically speaking)
that does not serve
Truth, Humanity, or this one and only Home.

Naked I and "I"

At first blush,

in the deep purple of dawn,

"I" awake to a naked I.

Surprise!

The air is cool against bare skin,

a thousand tiny droplets of dew

clinging to the blades of grass beneath.

"I" bow and say hello,

"How I have been waiting."

Naked I says,

"So good to see you!"

"So good to see you!"

And then, just laughter!

Like sunlight breaking through the clouds—

earth humming to the leaves brushing against

the morning light.

Just laughter.

Naked I and "I,"

bare, open,

laughing together.

A Voice

Sea shore,

Cliff edge,

Secret cave —

Murmur of birds,

Drumming rain,

Desert sands,

Gasping wind.

Outstretched limbs,

Kite strings,

Humming bees,

Mountain green,

Gushing brooks,

Smooth rocks —

Wave under wave,

Curl inside curl,

Fold after fold.

Refrain, refrain,

Refrain —

A voice is born

from these sounds,

from their pulse, their rhythm —

from the space in between,

the silent Aum,

where no-thing is added,

where all remains whole.

Refrain, refrain,

Refrain —

Until the silence sings.

Satsang Is…

…a hearth and
a welcome home
for all, including
all that is unwelcome.

…a spark
striking hard against
who you think you are,
like metal against flint.

…a flame
flickering and fluttering
like wings,
smoke trailing
like the tail of a kite,
everything that's hanging on
flapping and dancing loose—
the false stories, beliefs, and narratives;
the knee-jerk, yes-but responses;

the illusions of enlightenment;

the threadbare hopes of escape from

the messiness of emotion,

the paradox of life as a human.

...a sacred fire

of ignited and un-ignited

hearts

that light up

together.

Merging With the Ocean

Revelation Truth

This heart hears truth,

and is immediately

at ease,

immediately sees

the beauty,

immediately remembers

the ancient yearning,

and feels the fierce heat

of the sun of suns.

And how I burn,

brightly,

beyond belief,

beyond the capacity

to see

or be

seen.

What Is This?

Silence?

Mindless thoughts?

Stillness as yet unknown?

Have you really come to claim me?

Silence

Okay, I whisper.

And your lips bulge out to meet mine—

from inside the spaciousness.

The Last to Know

It shines from my eyes,
and I am the last to know.

It bursts from my chest,
and I am the last to know.

It hums in my ears,
and I am the last to know.

It dances in my bones,
and I am the last to know.

And then, I know.

Waiting and Seeing

What is trying to emerge in my life?

What gift is mine to share?

What is my purpose?

I hear Gangaji and Papaji say,

"Wait and See."

And so, in the meantime...

I dance and play,

invite friends to join,

and keep returning to breath's way,

living moments in their full array.

I stay here,

in the unbroken flow.

The questions no longer matter,

only "I" and "Here" remain,

naturally weaving together

all the true answers.

Never Bucket-less

At times I feel

empty,

at times I feel

full;

at times, I feel

nothing

is ever right.

I long to be emptied—

ready to spill,

more than eager to be filled—

ready to serve,

to serve the well

well.

I have been told

no one is bucket-less.

Our inner source does not run dry.

What would it be like

to pour forth, endlessly?

To water and nourish,

to be emptied

without loss,

to overflow

without end—

to never know

where I begin

or where I have already become?

There Comes a Time

There comes a time

when the only thing to "do"

is to know, once and for all,

that you are lodged

in the heart of your teacher,

in the heart of your teacher's teacher,

in the heart of your teacher's teacher's teacher…

There comes a time

when the only thing to "do"

is to be quiet, once and for all—

just be still,

like the space between heartbeats,

where time pauses,

and all sound fades into the background.

No more questions,

no more seeking,

no-thing to "do" but breathe in

the vast, unspoken silence.

Then, there comes a time

when you simply must

give your teacher(s) a break!

Let *Satguru* speak the truth:

"All teachers' hearts are lodged in your heart—

there is only One Heart.

There is only One.

And That One...

That is You."

Rumi and I

Rumi, here we are, you and I,

side by side.

The words that lived in your world,

come alive in mine now.

Your tongue touches mine,

your heart beats my heart.

Your hand finds my arm,

tugs, pulls me

into unfathomable

depths.

Awed, unmoored,

I pour into the scent of this rose,

the flow of this milk,

the juice of this peach,

and all other fruit.

I am snow in your hands,

helplessly melting into a

thirsty, thirsty source.

I drink and drink and drink—

not to quench, it seems,

but to keep this thirst going,

to keep this yearning alive,

to keep tasting more of holy water.

Oh, to be so immersed, so saturated,

so close that we naturally merge

into a single drop of bliss.

It is inexplicably simple:

Rumi and I have taken the plunge—

until no-thing does us part.

The Way of Grace

Nail your hands

to the cross

of longing,

toss your fears

into the ache

of your heart.

Close your palms

to the path of distraction,

and open them

to the way of grace—

a vigilance,

soft and steady,

in the ache

that knows.

Immeasurable Heaven

Here we are, together—

In Immeasurable Heaven.

Believe it or not,

Here we are:

Immeasurable Heaven.

Why then do some feel

Immeasurable Hell?

Life is not easy—

It chews us up,

spits us out into the abyss.

Yet always, there is This:

Immeasurable Heaven.

It simply Is.

And all you need

is willingness to fall—

not into despair, but into that place

that is yourself,

that "That"

that is

Immeasurable Heaven.

Closing Reflection

What a gift it is to pause.
To breathe.
To wake in joy.

These poems have been my offering,
a way of witnessing the vast stillness
that holds us all.

Footprints in sand.
Waves dissolving on the shore.
Echoes fading into silence.

And yet—silence remains.

I leave you here,
at the threshold of presence.

May you walk on with wonder.

May you listen deeply.

And may we meet ourselves,

again and again,

in the boundless love of being.

Inspirations

Gangaji, your Existence (p.11)

Inspired by a Dharma talk by Papaji, *Return to Silence*, Gangaji Foundation Video Library. Papaji says that wisdom will come searching for you, and find you where you have always been: *Home – in the holy company of Yourself.*

Refresh (p.25)

Inspired by clips from the video *What Happens When the Questions End?* 2016, Gangaji Foundation Video Library.

Deeper into Yourself (p. 60)

Inspired by *A Meeting with Gangaji*, Lake Tahoe, 2000, Gangaji Foundation Video Library. Gangaji words: *If you are willing to go off the edge of the earth, you will see that it is you yourself that holds the earth. And you cannot go off from yourself, you can only go deeper into yourself.*

This Wild Ride that is Life (p. 61)

Inspired by clips from the video *What Happens When the Questions End?* 2016, Gangaji Foundation Video Library.

Don't Go Worshipping Rainbows (p. 71)

Inspired by the video *The Secret of Surrender*, 1995, Gangaji Foundation Video Library. Gangaji invites us to see that the forms we love or worship are no less than our very own self shining back.

It's All a Love Affair (p. 72)

Inspired by Gangaji's words in a recording of Satsang, Byron Bay Retreat, 2006, Gangaji Foundation video library: *It's all a love affair, you know…* she says, and lists all that is *Still the Beloved.*

Grateful is Too Skinny a Word (p. 76)

Inspired by the phrase, *Grateful is too skinny a word* uttered by a participant in one of Gangaji's Satsangs as she expressed her deepest thanks.

There Comes a Time (p. 118)

Inspired by some clips in the video *What Happens When the Questions End?* 2016, Gangaji Foundation Video Library.

The Way of Grace (p. 122)

Inspired by clips from the video *The Secret of Surrender*, 1995, Gangaji Foundation Video Library and Gangaji's words: *Nail your own hands to the cross of longing* entered like an arrow, and then the poem simply emerged.

Immeasurable Heaven (p. 123)

Inspired (or prompted) by the two words *Immeasurable Heaven* spoken at the beginning of the recording from 2014, *Give the Silence a Chance*, Gangaji Foundation Video Library.

Acknowledgements

First and foremost, my deepest gratitude goes to my husband, Norbert, for his unwavering love, support, and companionship—the foundation of my journey.

To my sons, Kevin and Erik, thank you for being the incredible souls that you are. Your presence is a constant source of joy and inspiration.

Heartfelt appreciation to Barbara, Harriet, and Shanti, and to all those at the Gangaji Foundation who dedicate themselves to peace, freedom, and joy in the world. My gratitude also extends to the Foundation's extensive media library, beautiful member portal, and the spaces for connection—the forum, community pages, and all that is shared so generously.

To Sarah, Roos, and Tricia—thank you for your friendship and open hearts. Our shared conversations, creative exchanges, and presence in each other's lives are a true gift.

To my beloved sisters, Corinna, Nicola, and Julia, thank you for the bond we share, and for the quiet strength that continues to sustain me in countless ways.

Finally, with deep love and remembrance, I honour my parents, Karin and Derrick who, though no longer here, remain an integral part of who I am. Their love, guidance, and legacy live on in my heart and in all that I create.

Index of Poems

About the Author

 Diana Button is a poet and author whose work delves beneath the surface of what it means to be human. With a touch that is at once playful and profound, childlike and wise, her writing invites readers to say yes to life and discover the depth of their own unique nature. At the heart of her work lies the fundamental question: *Who am I?*

She is the author of *From Pen(elope) with Love xxx* (2020), a collection of poetry and prose, and *Marrying It All* (2003), a novel. Her poetry has also been featured in the anthologies *Writing from a Small Country* and *D'Waasser am Mond* (2004).

Beyond her writing, Diana actively engages with the Gangaji Foundation, particularly in their Prison Program. Her work has appeared in *Freedom Inside*, a newsletter that is part of Gangaji's Self-Inquiry course for incarcerated individuals across the United States.

Residing in Germany with her husband of thirty-five years, Diana draws inspiration from the natural world, the voices of Rumi, Hafiz, and

Kahlil Gibran, and the teachings of Gangaji and Papaji—wisdom passed down through the lineage of awakening and self-inquiry from Ramana Maharshi.

Rooted in silence, these teachings call her to rest in the unbroken stillness of being, reminding her to release striving, shed illusions, and uncover joy—not as an experience, but as her (as our) true essence and birthright.